Haiku on Ice

by

Margaret C. Wang

1663 Liberty Drive, Suite 200
Bloomington, Indiana 47403
(800) 839-8640
www.AuthorHouse.com

© 2005 Margaret C. Wang
All Rights Reserved.

No part of this book may be reproduced, stored in a retrieval system, or transmitted by any means without the written permission of the author.

First published by AuthorHouse 05/20/05

ISBN: 1-4208-0773-0 (e)
ISBN: 1-4208-0772-2 (sc)

Library of Congress Control Number: 2004098632

Printed in the United States of America
Bloomington, Indiana

This book is printed on acid-free paper.

Haiku on Ice

With cold air blowing
My ponytail flying
Me, happy on the ice.

Margaret C. Wang

Fun in the rink

Judges are superfluous

Placement is extra.

Haiku on Ice

Quality with speed
Smiling at the boist'rous crowd
Jumping to the beat.

Margaret C. Wang

Jumping with landings
Applause fills the arena
A beautiful place.

Haiku on Ice

Crowds cheering you on
Pushing until the ending
Gliding to your pose.

Margaret C. Wang

Free to go away

Like birds flying to their homes

Knowing this freedom.

Haiku on Ice

Feeling the music
Capturing the breeze
Skating 'cross the arena.

Margaret C. Wang

Freedom and delight
Enjoying the artistry
Out there by yourself.

Haiku on Ice

Your name is announced

Stepping out to your pose

Your dream is waiting.

Margaret C. Wang

The colored lights

At "Ice Chips"

Memories for me forever.

The costumes, the lights
Ready for fun to begin
The spotlight is set.

Margaret C. Wang

The day: your triumph
It's the best you can do
To be a champion.

Haiku on Ice

Gliding to your spot.
Enjoying every moment
Adding to the fun.

Margaret C. Wang

The magic of ice

Glistening in the light

Floating to the song.

Solidly landing

The jump while creating deep edges

Gaining power.

Margaret C. Wang

Achieving the finish
Best wishes with delight
The challenge is done!

Haiku on Ice

Play the music again
Building muscle memory
Over and over.

Margaret C. Wang

Step sequence with jumps
Away in the air of fun
Learning with coaches.

Haiku on Ice

Golden memories

Forever in your mind's rink

Skate for more and more.

Margaret C. Wang

The freezing cold air
With everyone in the stands
You're watching you smile.

Relaxing your mind's eye
Before your competition
Believe in yourself.

Margaret C. Wang

Prepare for the day

Skating with your heart and soul

Concentrating now.

Haiku on Ice

Release and joy, skating
Jumping and spinning
My sport my freedom.

Margaret C. Wang

Training to compete

Working hard and having fun

Capturing the speed.

Haiku on Ice

Silence but the ice
Scratching zen into my soul
Just me and the white.

Margaret C. Wang

Into the cold ice

My blade digs into circles

Out comes a waltz eight

Haiku on Ice

The best of the best
Performing with ease and power
Joy with glory.

Margaret C. Wang

Pushing and speeding

Taking off on a deep edge in the air

Then, "check out."

Haiku on Ice

I glide smoothly and
Attempt a jump with great ease
I fall with full speed.

Margaret C. Wang

Forward or backward
In the beginning, I fell
But now, I can skate.

Haiku on Ice

Swizzle and twizzle
You skate with frequent
Wobbles and giggles.

Margaret C. Wang

You look back

At these moments

Now, happily grinning with pride.

Haiku on Ice

Toes pointed

fingertips elegantly turned

Blades crisscrossing the ice.

Margaret C. Wang

Mazurka, skip

Blue skies overhead sun ablaze

Forever flying.

Haiku on Ice

High over the ice

I jump

I land and I glide freely for a while.

Margaret C. Wang

Three turn waltz eight

Mohawk Choctaw

I love them all when I skate today.

Haiku on Ice

My feet tap, twinkle,

Swish, crunch, step

On the ice, I create a program.

Margaret C. Wang

Age five I began

Now I am fourteen

Hydroblading in my soul.

Haiku on Ice

The purest circle
Edge clever and elusive
I try but I fall.

Margaret C. Wang

Helmet, snowsuit, mittens
Bursting with excitement
Your first step and fall.

Haiku on Ice

Earn what you deserve
A reward or not, I say
Just smile, jump, spin, win.

Margaret C. Wang

Inspired by TV
Music, lights, sequins
Skates, hot chocolate and ice.

Age five, Taylor

My best friend and I

Starting our first steps on the ice.

Margaret C. Wang

Power crossovers

High I leap

Double axel I will conquer you.

Haiku on Ice

Checkout they say
I can't fast enough, I say
Do it until you can.

Margaret C. Wang

I can't. I say

Yes, they say and by gosh, I do it

Ta da! I can.

Haiku on Ice

Hold the leg higher

But I can't again

Yes they say and then I do.

Margaret C. Wang

Try harder they say

I am too exhausted now

Then I land and stand.

Haiku on Ice

Breaking a toe
Or two, I'm back on the ice
Really so glad to skate.

Margaret C. Wang

It's a gift of time

To skate with abandon here

To find my freedom.

Haiku on Ice

Soon I will be too
Busy to skate and fly
Just do it today.

Margaret C. Wang

The best is now.

Whiteness the cold ice.

Blue steel sends me high in the air.

Haiku on Ice

Speed power I love
The clarity of the air
Yes. I jump for me

Margaret C. Wang

The chill in the rink
I sweat, I race and I fly
I land my axel.

Haiku on Ice

Three turn, triple toe

Double toe

Nothing stops my exhilaration.

Margaret C. Wang

My breath is hot
I sweat, I spin and I check out
And I end sweetly.

Haiku on Ice

I balance on an edge

Like my life

Don't fall too hard, so far so good.

Margaret C. Wang

Tipping over now,
An instant, I like the risk
Ice is on my side.

Haiku on Ice

Ten thousand double axels
They say I must do
In the end, I did.

Margaret C. Wang

What a sport: sequins
Sweat, hard work, blisters
I miss it when I can't skate.

Haiku on Ice

All of us, competitors
for ten years and more
Now friends totally.

Margaret C. Wang

Competing

Winning Losing

Now I just skate because it's part of me.

Haiku on Ice

Soft flute strains,
Crescendo, pianissimo
The blade is my instrument.

Margaret C. Wang

Sequins pretty and
Colors divine, power quick
Nothing quite like it.

Haiku on Ice

The white ice canvas

Asks me to risk

Then I jump and land to applause.

Margaret C. Wang

The cool chilly air greets me

Six in the morning

Makes me want to skate

Haiku on Ice

Ice crystals nipping
Firmly at my blade's edge
Crunch, stop suddenly.

Margaret C. Wang

Sunlight streaming on the ice

Prisms of color

As I glide to you.

Haiku on Ice

Split jump, hands touching my toes
Arms high over my boots
Boy was it fun.

Margaret C. Wang

Shall we skate, you, me
Together on the ice, in the sun
Fast and free?

Haiku on Ice

Indescribable
Aloft in the air never landing
Like a bird.

Margaret C. Wang

The short program

Full of expectation and thrill

Of the tricks on blades

Haiku on Ice

Evoking , stroking, feeling
I dance on an ice crystal
Flying, speeding

Margaret C. Wang

First I prepare my mind

Step on center ice, pause,

Wind up and let go.

Haiku on Ice

In my little world

Expressing all feelings, good and bad

Boundless, energized.

Margaret C. Wang

Zamboni surfaced ice
Like a magic carpet
I transform myself.

Haiku on Ice

Emotion and control
I enjoy being myself
Exploring me on edge.

Margaret C. Wang

Energy with ice
Until you become white hot
On thin metal blades.

Haiku on Ice

Deep outside edge
Kick off from one toe
Into the air, feeling the high.

Margaret C. Wang

It is exercise

For fun, clearing your bad thoughts

Relax and don't think!

Haiku on Ice

Being in control,

Use your imagination!

Relaxing with hope.

Margaret C. Wang

Believing in me
Working so hard to achieve
Striving for the best!

Haiku on Ice

Medal or no medal

I love to skate

Smiling at the boistr'ous crowd.

Printed in the United States
35158LVS00007B/268-288